Trust Me, JACK'S BEANSTALK STINKS!

The Story of JACK AND THE BEANSTALK as Told by THE GIANT

by Eric Braun
illustrated by Cristian Bernardini

PICTURE WINDOW BOOKS
a capstone imprint

Special thanks to our adviser, Terry Flaherty, PhD, Professor of English, Minnesota State University, Mankato, for his expertise.

Editor: Jill Kalz
Designer: Lori Bye
Art Director: Nathan Gassman
Production Specialist: Sarah Bennett
The illustrations in this book were created digitally.

Picture Window Books
1710 Roe Crest Drive
North Mankato, MN 56003
www.capstonepub.com

Library of Congress Cataloging-in-Publication Data
Braun, Eric, 1971–
Trust me, Jack's beanstalk stinks! : the story of Jack and the beanstalk as told by the giant / written by Eric Braun ; illustrated by Cristian Bernardini.
p. cm. — (The other side of the story)
Summary: The giant tells what really happened when Jack kept climbing up the beanstalk and sneaking into his house.
ISBN 978-1-4048-6675-1 (library binding)
ISBN 978-1-4048-7050-5 (paperback)
[1. Fairy tales. 2. Humorous stories.] I. Bernardini, Cristian, 1975– ill. II. Title.
PZ8.B6732Tr 2012
[E]—dc22 2011006996

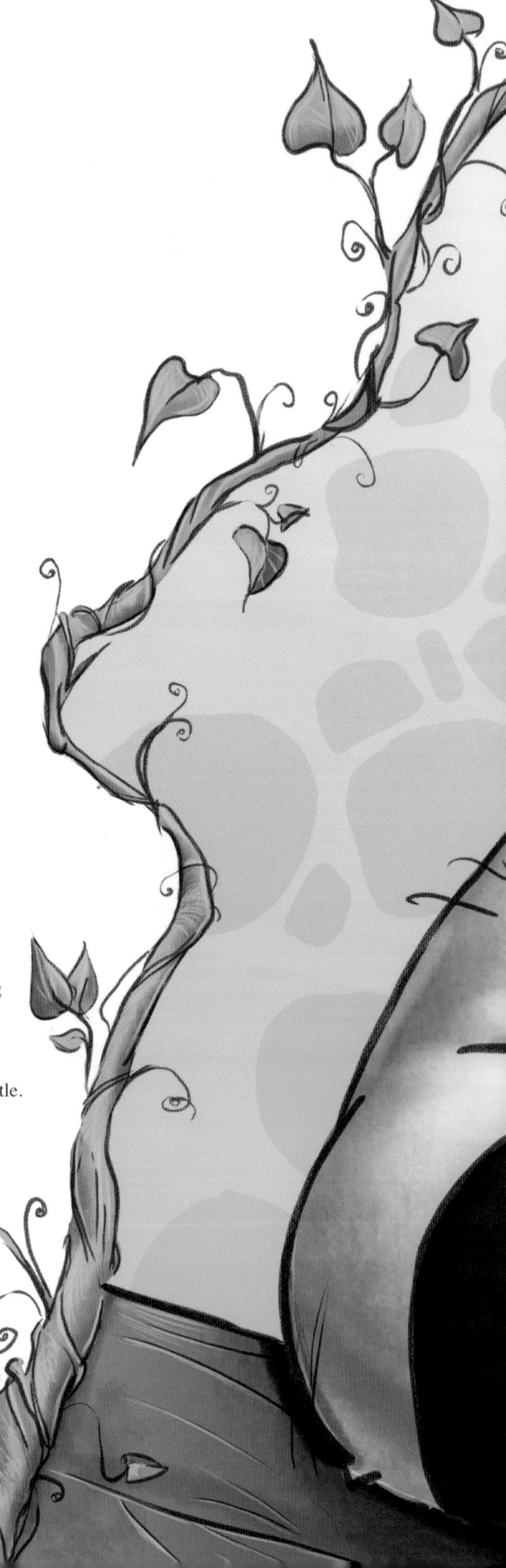

Printed in the United States of America in North Mankato, Minnesota.
112016 010160R

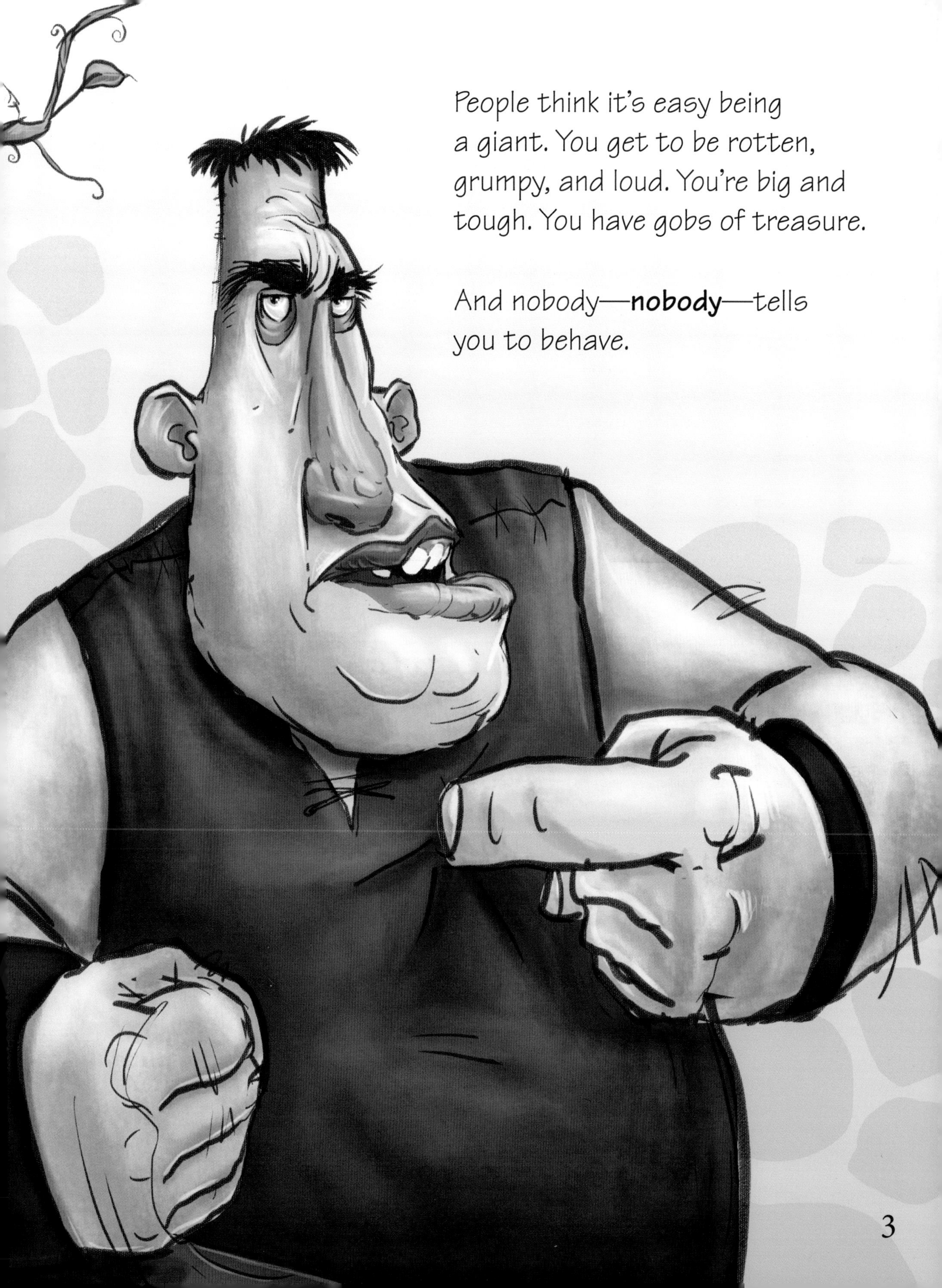

People think it's easy being a giant. You get to be rotten, grumpy, and loud. You're big and tough. You have gobs of treasure.

And nobody—**nobody**—tells you to behave.

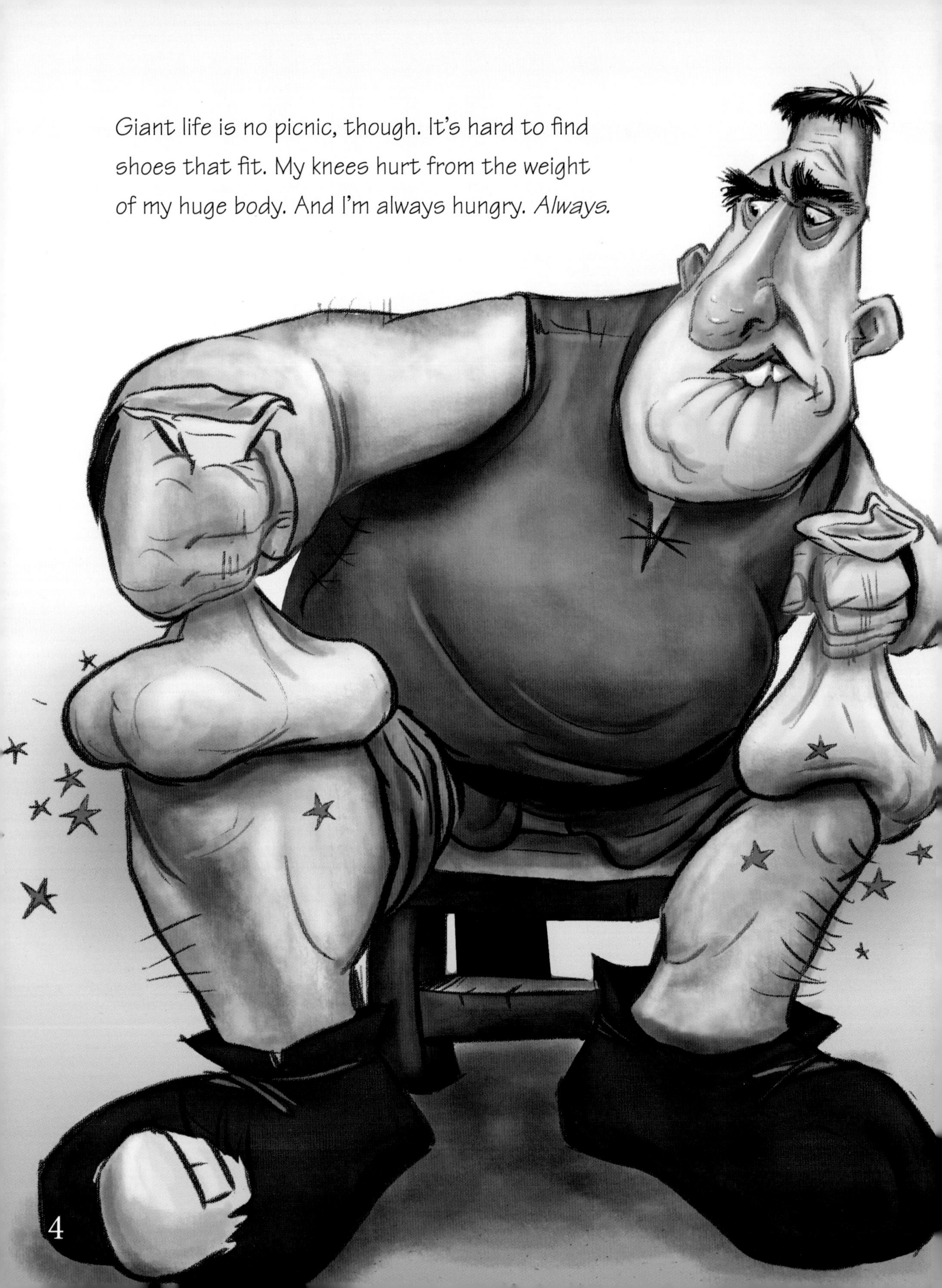

Giant life is no picnic, though. It's hard to find shoes that fit. My knees hurt from the weight of my huge body. And I'm always hungry. *Always.*

But the worst thing? *Humans.*

Humans are part of a balanced giant breakfast. But when you're not eating them, they're a real pain. Sometimes they laugh at me behind my back. They call me "stinky" and "fatso." They ring my doorbell and run away. Ha ha ha, very funny!

This boy named Jack was extra bold. He came up through the clouds one day while I was out gathering a small breakfast. He tricked my wife into feeding him, then hid inside my house. I mean, come on. Would he hide inside a *human's* house? That's a crime!

WELCOME TO OUR HOME!

Well, he didn't trick me. I could smell him.
(He smelled delicious.)
Maybe you still smell that Kiddie Kasserole from supper last night.

"FEE, FI, FO, FUM!"

I said. In Giant, this means something like "Go on home now. I promise I won't eat you."

But he stayed in his hiding place, the little rat.

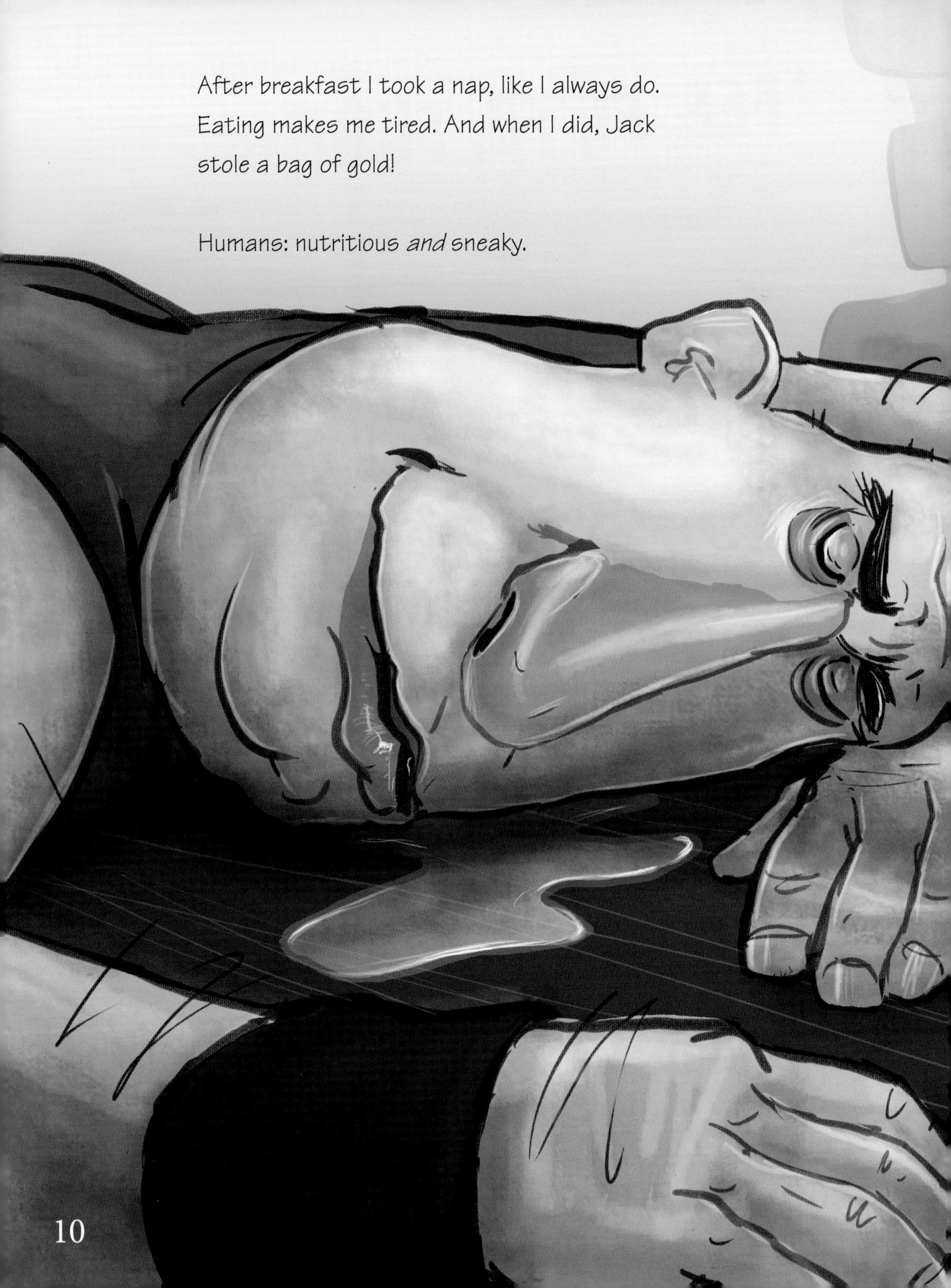

After breakfast I took a nap, like I always do. Eating makes me tired. And when I did, Jack stole a bag of gold!

Humans: nutritious *and* sneaky.

Some time later, Jack came back again. And again, he tricked my wife into letting him inside.

When I came home from picking up a light breakfast, I could smell him. I knew who it was.

"FEE, FI, FO, FUM!"

I yelled. This can also mean "Give me back my gold, and we'll call it even. I definitely won't eat you."

But he didn't come out.

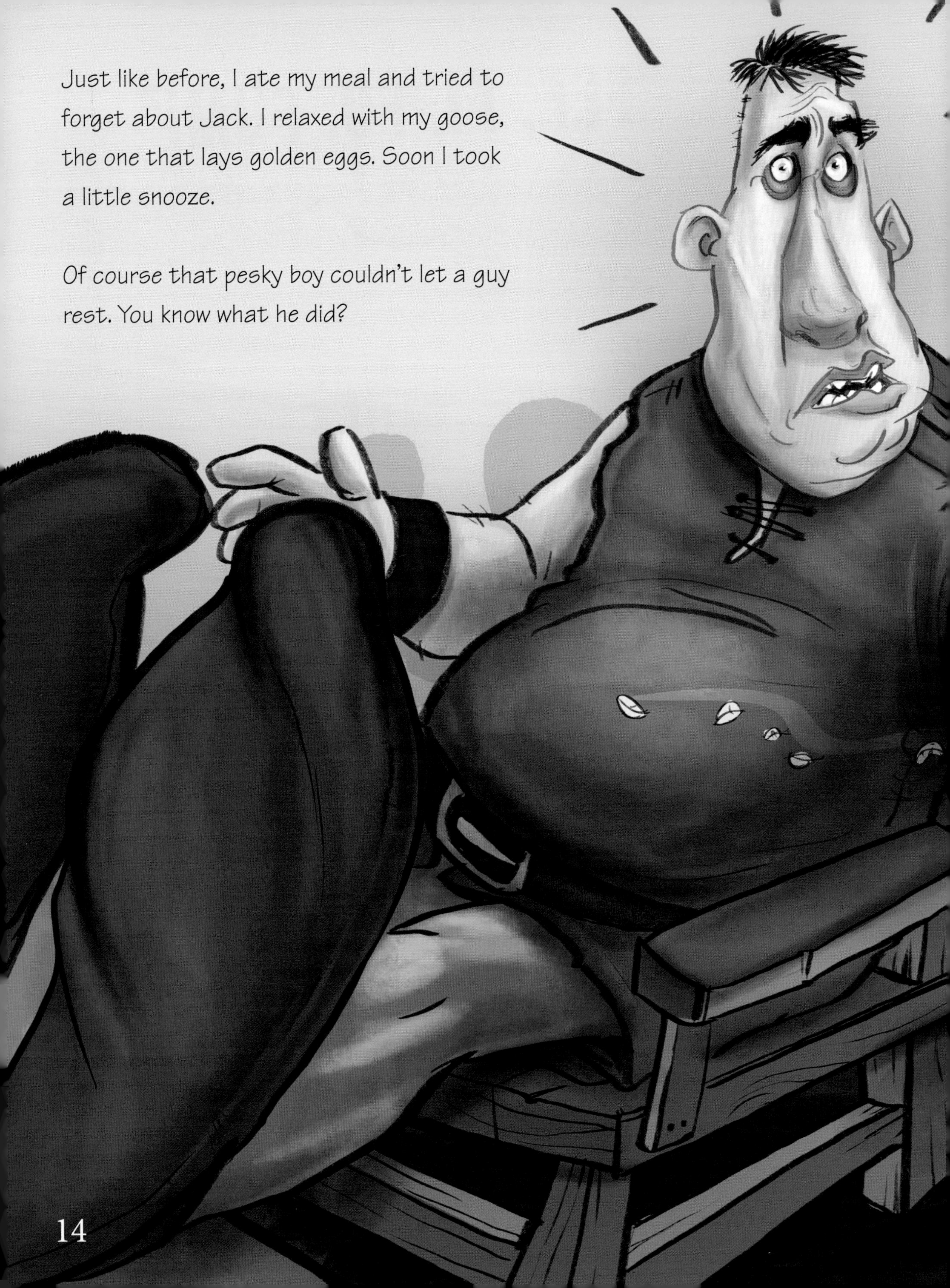

Just like before, I ate my meal and tried to forget about Jack. I relaxed with my goose, the one that lays golden eggs. Soon I took a little snooze.

Of course that pesky boy couldn't let a guy rest. You know what he did?

HE *STOLE* *MY GOOSE*, THE LOUSY, NO-GOOD, MISERABLE THIEF!

The last time Jack came around, I called out,

"FEE, FI, FO, FUM!"

This can even mean "Darn it, I'm really angry now!"

My wife and I searched but couldn't find him. I kept looking, but soon I got hungry. (Big surprise.)

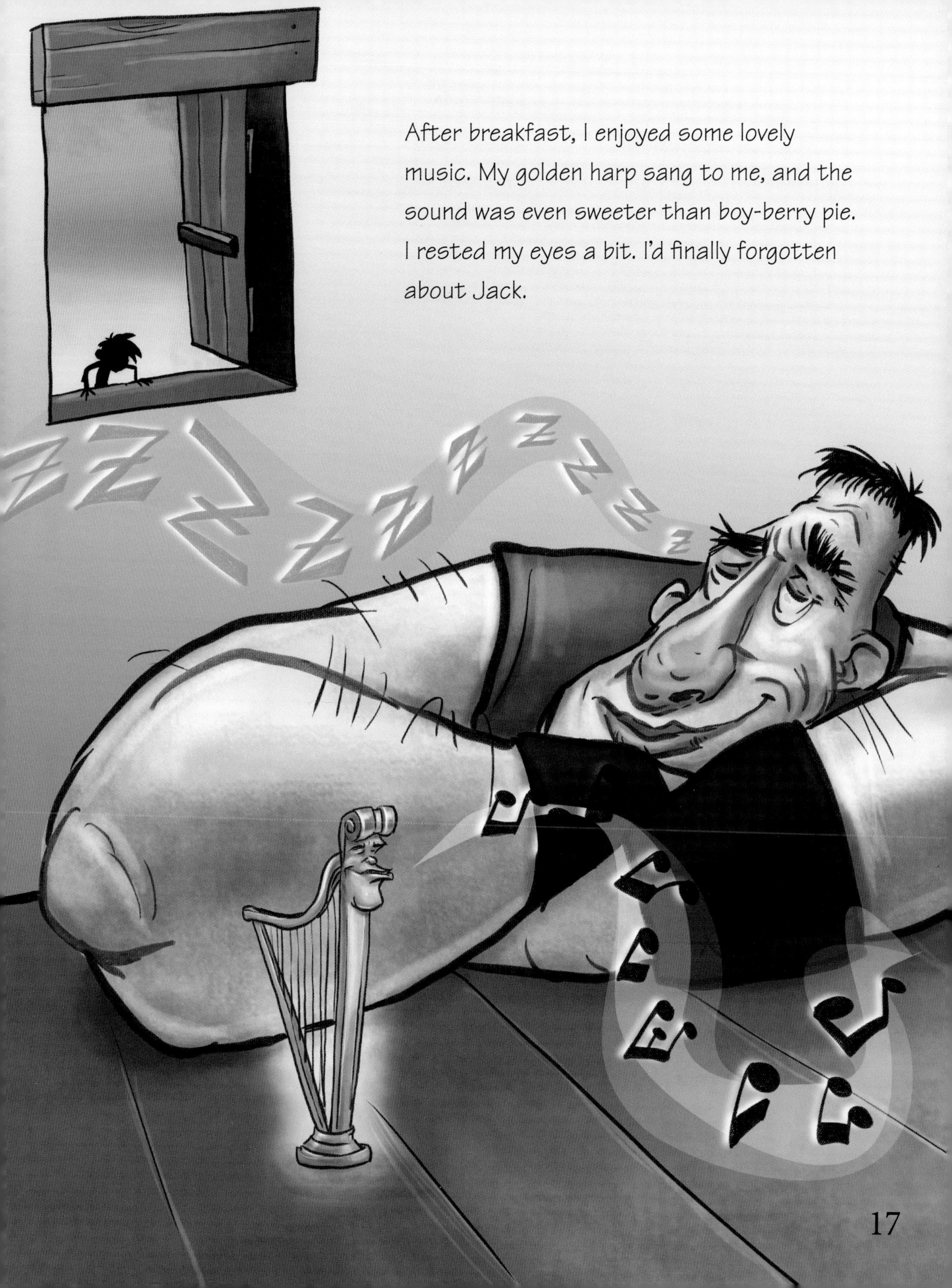

After breakfast, I enjoyed some lovely music. My golden harp sang to me, and the sound was even sweeter than boy-berry pie. I rested my eyes a bit. I'd finally forgotten about Jack.

The next thing you know, my harp is calling, "Master! Master!" Jack was running off with it, and I thundered after. I almost caught up to them, too, but they disappeared into the clouds.

And there it was: a big beanstalk. Jack was climbing down it.

Well, I'm a smart guy. I know a dangerous thing when I see it. I didn't want to go down there. No way! But then my harp called out again.

So down I went. Down, down …
That stalk was wobbly.
But I kept going.

The beanstalk shook once, twice, then toppled over. Jack had chopped it with an ax! I fell and broke my crown. That's an old-fashioned way of saying I whacked my head real good.

Even if you're a big, tough giant, that hurts.

My wife said I should forget about Jack. But sometimes I still look through the hole in the clouds.

Jack and his mother got rich selling golden eggs. They fattened up nicely. And Jack got married. My golden harp sang at the wedding. It was a lovely party.

I'll tell you one thing. Someday, when my crown feels better, I'm going down there to get my stuff back. Maybe I'll grab lunch while I'm there too.

Think About It

Read a classic version of *Jack and the Beanstalk* and compare it to the giant's version. List some things that happen in the classic version that don't happen in the giant's version. Why do you think those parts were left out of the giant's story?

The classic version of *Jack and the Beanstalk* is told by an invisible narrator. This version is told by the giant, from the giant's point of view. How might the story be different if it were told from another character's point of view? What if Jack, Jack's mother, or the giant's wife told the story?

The classic version of the story lets readers know that Jack and his mom are very poor and hungry. The giant's version doesn't talk about that. How does leaving out this information change the story?

The giant says it's hard to be a giant. Humans bother him, and he just wants to be left alone. Do you believe him? Why or why not?

Glossary

character—a person, animal, or creature in a story

narrator—a person who tells a story

point of view—a way of looking at something

version—an account of something from a certain point of view

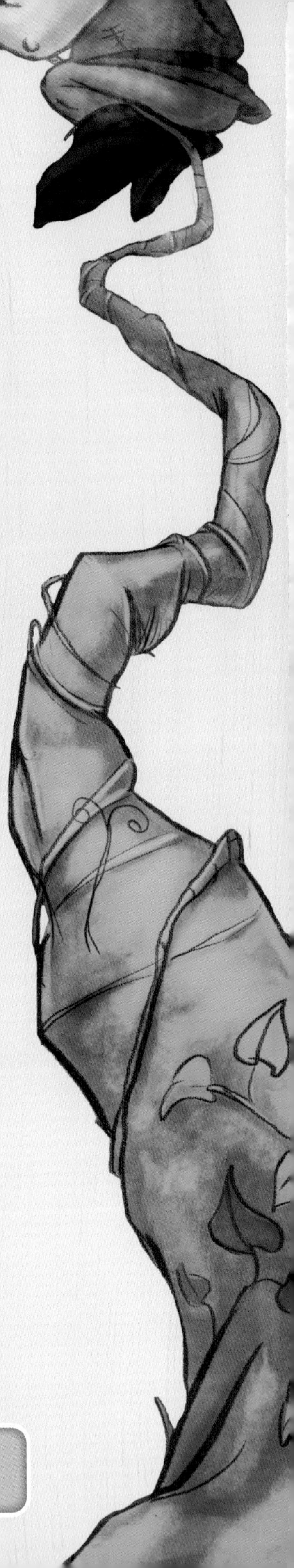

Read More

Cech, John, retold by. *Jack and the Beanstalk.* New York: Sterling Pub. Co., 2008.

Hoena, Blake A. *Jack and the Beanstalk: The Graphic Novel.* Graphic Spin. Mankato, Minn.: Stone Arch Books, 2009.

Lynette, Rachel. *Ogres.* Monsters. Detroit: KidHaven Press, 2010.

Internet Sites

FactHound offers a safe, fun way to find Internet sites related to this book. All of the sites on FactHound have been researched by our staff.

Here's all you do:

Visit *www.facthound.com*

Type in this code: 9781404866751

Look for all the books in the series:

Believe Me, Goldilocks Rocks!

Honestly, Red Riding Hood Was Rotten!

Seriously, Cinderella Is SO Annoying!

Trust Me, Jack's Beanstalk Stinks!